# Brave Little Beasts

## Contents

Bertie Dragon Bakes a Pie
Page 2

Teach a Griffin How to Fly
Page 9

Poems by Wendy Meddour
Illustrated by Stephanie Laberis
and Agnes Baruzzi

They like to roar and spit out flames. They try hard to be bad.

But Bertie Dragon liked to bake.
He liked to dance and sing.

He was a happy dragon,
Not a sad and grumpy thing.

The king said, "No, of course not. We need dragons that can play!"

Bertie was so happy that
He flew into the sky.
Then he sang a dragon song
And he made a dragon pie.

# Teach a Griffin How to Fly

The griffin was a silly bird
He could not get it right.
When he tried to flap his wings,
He looked a silly sight.

He crashed into a bush.

Then he crashed into the sea!

"I think that you can do it!"
Said a tiny little mouse.
"A griffin should not be feeling sad
Inside his griffin house."

And so the griffin tried until ...

he flew like all the rest.

The mouse jumped on his back and said, "Griffin, you're the BEST!"